T0380634

Three
Dimensions
of Prayer

Three Dimensions of Prayer

A One-Year Intercessory Prayer Tool

Dr. Shelia R. Lewis

ARCHWAY
PUBLISHING

Unless otherwise indicated, all scriptures are taken from the King James Version, public domain.

Scripture quotations marked MSG are taken from THE MESSAGE, copyright © 1993, 2002, 2018 by Eugene H. Peterson. Used by permission of NavPress. All rights reserved. Represented by Tyndale House Publishers, Inc.

Archway Publishing books may be ordered through booksellers or by contacting:

Archway Publishing
1663 Liberty Drive
Bloomington, IN 47403
www.archwaypublishing.com
844-669-3957

Because of the dynamic nature of the Internet, any web addresses or links contained in this book may have changed since publication and may no longer be valid. The views expressed in this work are solely those of the author and do not necessarily reflect the views of the publisher, and the publisher hereby disclaims any responsibility for them.

Any people depicted in stock imagery provided by Getty Images are models, and such images are being used for illustrative purposes only.
Certain stock imagery © Getty Images.

Praying hands concept by
Bishop Stephen Patterson
http://stephenepatterson.com/index2.html

Praying hands and archangel artwork by
Godwin Sorianosos
gsorianosos@gmail.com

ISBN: 978-1-6657-5864-2 (sc)
ISBN: 978-1-6657-5865-9 (e)

Library of Congress Control Number: 2024906445

Print information available on the last page.

Archway Publishing rev. date: 09/06/2024

Angel Defeating Satan

This is no afternoon athletic contest that we'll walk away from and forget about in a couple of hours. This is for keeps, a life-or-death fight to the finish against the Devil and all his angels...prayer is essential in this ongoing warfare. Pray hard and long. Pray for your brothers and sisters. Keep your eyes open. Keep each other's spirits up so that no one falls behind or drops out.

Ephesians 6:12 and 18 (The Message Bible)

Praying Hands

If my people, which are called by my name, shall humble themselves, and pray, and seek my face, and turn from their wicked ways, then will I hear from heaven, and will forgive their sin, and will heal their land.

2 Chronicles 7:14 (KJV)

Contents

Introduction

Prayer is a way of asking God for things we desire, according to His will. Asking entails action on our part. The acrostic **A–S–K** speaks for itself, where "**A**" is Ask, "**S**" is seek and "**K**" is knock. Matthew 7:7 and Philippians 4:6 encourage us to ask (beg/plead) God and seek, as in a deep search, for His presence (answer). Our ultimate goal is to strike the mark God wants us to, according to His will and avoid praying amiss.

Although we are taught to pray, few have taken the time to pray effective prayers. Prayer is such a profound action that one of Jesus' disciples asked Him to teach them all to pray (Luke 11:1). Although Jesus CALLED (divinely selected or appointed) the disciples, the miracles and evident manifestations of Jesus' prayers encouraged the disciples to want to have that same type of communion with the Heavenly Father. Like the disciples, we must be prayer warriors and commune daily with God.

Through prayer, we develop a dialogue with our Father that leads to thanksgiving, praise and an opportunity to be still and hear Him.

This one-year intercessory prayer is only a tool. Continuous prayer will help you draw closer to God and ultimately pray effectively and fervently, yielding to His desired results. Hence, the scriptural foundational text within this series is based upon:

(a) Three dimensions of prayer[1]: supplications, prayers, and intercessions (1 Timothy 2:1), and
(b) God's stated desires in 2 Chronicles 7:14.

---

[1] In assuming the posture of prayer, believers must first forgive others so God can forgive our sins. In other words, we need a clean slate from God (Mark 11:25, The Message), so that our prayers are effective.

Prayer Definitions According to 1 Timothy 2:1

Supplication

Supplication is prayer that seeks benefits of God or man. In 1 Timothy 2:1, it means to specifically seek the favor (benefits) of God for oneself and or another's great need. Ephesians 6:18 supports this when Paul exhorts us to pray with "all prayer and *supplication in the Spirit*." In essence, supplication is PRAYING for what is beneficial, according to God's desire (Jesus alludes to this in Luke 11:2 stating "Thy kingdom come, Thy *will* be done...").

Prayer

Prayer is asking. Once we plead or entreat God for His will through supplication, then we ask for what He desires us to pray, "for we know not what we should pray for as we ought" (Rom 8:26). Amazingly, because we sought His will first, we are placed in a Holy position to allow His desires to become our desires. Prayer in this sense is not only the "asking," but Holy positioning through various kinds of prayer, not limited to but includes confession, adoration, and humble prostration. Remember, in 2 Chronicles 7:14 God tells us to "humble ourselves, pray, and seek His face."

Intercession

Intercession is most often associated with praying the hedge or standing in the gap for others (Ez 22:30; Jer 27:18; I Sam 12:23; Luke 11:5-8). However, intercession is also what we *do* based on what the Intercessor (Jesus) sends us, from the Holy Office of Intercession (Rom 8:26-27, 34). It is imperative that we cooperate with the Holy Spirit so that we become receptive to the moves Jesus sends, such as praise, thanksgiving, dancing, praying, etc. In other words, Jesus provides us with *actions* that INTERCEPT the fiery darts of the enemy, and we merely operate (intercede) in His finished works.

Giving of Thanks be Made for All Men

As with all prayer, we must believe that what we prayed is accomplished. This is reasonable since we prayed the Words of God. Because we know what we ask is answered, we give God thanks for our "right now" answered prayer. We can also give God thanks for all men because it's through *relationships* of others that God answers our prayers, i.e., the appointed doctor to contribute to a prayer of healing, favor from a judge in a legal matter, and the list goes on.

Overall, to efficiently and effectively operate in the finished works, we must do as Jesus did, which is to seek the Father's face by humbling ourselves and spending time in prayer. Then, when we exit the prayer closet, whether at our place of worship or in our living rooms, we will know:

(a) We had a shared encounter with our Father and He heard us,
(b) Our sins are forgiven, and
(c) Whatever we prayed for is made whole (complete).

Now let's humble ourselves and seek His Holy presence!!!

How to Use this Tool

There are no formulas or scientific methods for praying to God for prayers we want answered. Your relationship with God is personal. This section explains how to get the most out of the one-year intercessory prayer tool.

This one-year intercessory prayer tool contains 12 sections, one for each month.

These sections are designed to assist in disciplining your heart to become grounded in the Word of God, as you pray. Each section represents one month and is broken down into weeks. Monthly topics are briefly paraphrased, for effectual prayer, followed by scriptural reading, text and "For the Closet," which is a secret place that you designate for your prayer life. The weekly text and scripture provide the supportive Word of God for the topic, and "For the Closet" illuminates the scripture for the week, as you pray.

As you journey through this tool, day-by-day, expect a dialogue with God, as you seek His presence through prayer. A notes section appears at the conclusion of each month, for you to record and journal Divine revelation. These reflective notes should be based on your encounters with God, as they unfold.

Before you begin to pray the weekly scriptures, provided in each section, take a little time to read these scriptures in their full context. This may require you to read scriptures before and after the selected scripture(s), or read the entire chapter, to obtain full knowledge of the intent of the inspired Words of God.

For example, God's Words in 2 Chronicles 7:14 is often used for a prayer of humility to God, repentance, acknowledging that God hears, answers, and heals. To put this scripture in full context, you would first have to read 2 Chronicles 16:12-42, which provides a background of Solomon's prayer of dedication of the temple to God and supplication for Israel. Then, read 2 Chronicles 7:12-22 to reveal:

(a) God's response to Solomon's dedication of the temple and supplication for Israel,
(b) An established covenant between God and Solomon, and
(c) God telling Solomon He heard his prayer and intends to honor it.

Therefore, understanding the context of scripture helps us to understand God in a personal nature, as we enter the closet (secret place), and pray the Words of each weeks' scripture.

For example, if we "do" what God tells us to do in 2 Chronicles 7:14a, we can then pray "Father, as you heard Solomon, I know you have heard me, forgave me, and have healed my land" (i.e. healed my body, made my family whole, etc.). Then, believe by faith in Him that the prayer is "forever settled in Heaven" (Psalm 119:89).

Monthly Intercessory Prayer Topics Table

The following table is an overview of each month, along with the covered topic and the associated scripture(s).

*Month	Topic	Scripture(s)
1	Praying God's Will: Complete Submission to His Will	• 2 Chron 7:14 • Luke 11:2 • Psalm 119:89 • Mark 14:36
2	Aligned With the Word: Supplications, Prayers, Intercessions, and Thanksgiving	• Psalm 27:8 • Eph 6:18 • Rom 8:26–27 • Ps 100:4
3	New Beginnings: Our Beginnings in Him (Jesus Christ)	• I Chron 17:9 • Lam 3:21–23 • John 1:1–2, 14 • Rev 1:8
4	Revelation of Christ: Wisdom, Understanding & Knowledge	• Matt 16:16–17 • Eph 1:17–18 • 1 Cor 2:16 • Heb 13:8
5	Passion of Christ: God's Will in Action	• Luke 4:18–19 • Luke 22:42 & 44 • Acts 1:3 • Rom 10:9–10

*Month	Topic	Scripture(s)
6	Healing & Wholeness: Faith in God is Wholeness for God's People	• Is 53:5 • James 5:14–16 • Matt 14:35–36 • 1 Thess 5:23–25
7	Heaviness: Replaced With the Oil of Joy, Comforter & the Garment of Praise	• Ps 119:28 • Is 61:3 • John 14:15–18 • 1 Pet 1:5–7
8	Unnecessary Weight: Exercising Spiritual Liberty	• Hebrews 12:1(b) • Gal 2:4 • Heb 2:14(b)–15 • 1 John 4:4
9	Overcoming Idleness: Praying for a Fervent Spirit	• Isaiah 60:1 • Acts 18:25 • Rom 12:11–12 • Heb 6:12
10	Humility: Praying With an Humble Spirit	• 2 Chron 7:14 • Is 57:15 • Matt 18:4 • Pet 5:6–7
11	Leadership: Ensamples to the flock	• Josh 5:13(b) –14 • Matt 15:14 • Heb 13:7–8 • 1 Pet 5:2–3
12	Blessings for the children	• Gen 22:17–18 • Prov 20:7 • Acts 3:25 • Mark 10:14(b)–16

*If a month has more than four weeks, the fifth week's prayer will reflect scriptures from your Holy Man or Woman of God's most recent sermon. For example, if this individual speaks of forgiveness, revisit the scripture from that message and pray for God to provide you with a deeper revelation on this topic for yourself and others.

MONTH 1

Praying God's Will: Complete Submission to His Will

In the first month, you will enter the prayer closet (secret place), emptying yourself, and asking God to reveal His desire for you through prayer. In the months that follow, allow the scriptural texts to guide you into His presence by submitting to His Word, and praying those same Words into His glorious manifestation.

Week	Scripture	Text
1	2 Chronicles 7:14	If my people, which are called by my name, shall humble themselves, and pray, and seek My face, and turn from their wicked ways; then will I hear from heaven, and will forgive their sin, and will heal their land.

For the Closet: God chose and called us by His name; we didn't do anything to earn it. Upon accepting this love, freely bestowed, we must know that God wants us to humble ourselves and turn away from the things that are unlike Him. In this, we seek His Holy presence, invoking Him to hear our prayer, forgive us for turning away from Him, and then He will heal the broken things in our lives.

Week	Scripture	Text
2	Luke 11:2	And He said unto them, When ye pray, say, Our Father which art in heaven, Hallowed be Thy name. Thy kingdom come. Thy will be done, as in heaven, so in earth.

For the Closet: Jesus taught his disciples: (a) To recognize that God is *our* Father, (b) That His name is Holy and His kingdom is sovereign, (c) That we pray for the Father's will manifested in our lives, and (d) Not to pray for our own selfish purpose(s). Allow God to lead us in prayer, as Jesus did for His disciples.

Week	Scripture	Text
3	Psalm 119:89	For ever, O LORD, Thy word is settled in heaven.

For the Closet: Be it written or spoken, God's Word will not be moved! Therefore, it doesn't matter what things appear in the earthly realm; we can trust in the immoveable Word of God.

Week	Scripture	Text
4	Mark 14:36	And he said, Abba, Father, all things are possible unto thee; take away this cup from me: nevertheless not what I will, but what thou wilt.

For the Closet: When our souls are troubled, it is easy to pray for God to remove the things that trouble us. Mature Christians have developed a relationship with God that submits to His will, understanding that Father knows what is best for us and/or the situation we are praying for.

NOTES

_____

_____

_____

_____

_____

_____

_____

_____

_____

_____

_____

_____

_____

_____

_____

_____

MONTH 2

Aligned with the Word: Supplications, Prayers, Intercessions and Thanksgiving

Paul explains in 1 Timothy 2:1-8, it is God's desire that all men are saved—janitors, substance abusers, rich, and poor alike. Through prayer, we plead the cause for salvation of mankind and in the process cooperate with the leading of the Holy Spirit, which leads us to the Father, through the mediator Jesus Christ. Consequently, we can thank God for the salvation of mankind, and giving us peace, with all men, as we exit the prayer closet, in the knowledge that God has just answered His own prayers through His willing vessels—Us!

Week	Scripture	Text
1	Psalm 27:8	When thou saidst, Seek ye My face; My heart said unto thee, Thy face, LORD, will I seek.
For the Closet: We must seek the presence of God, but it first must be settled in the very core of our hearts. Remember, God searches the heart, so if *it* is settled, then we won't miss His presence.		

Dr. Shelia R. Lewis

Week	Scripture	Text
2	Ephesians 6:18	Praying always, with all prayer and supplication in the Spirit, and watching thereunto with all perseverance and supplication for all saints

For the Closet: Passages prior to this one define the armor of God that we must receive to stand against the enemy's devices. However, the armor is effective for its intended use, when we pray all prayers according to the will of God. As suited warriors fit for the fight and grounded in prayer, we also have the power to diligently pray for Godly boldness for our fellow prayer warriors.

Week	Scripture	Text
3	Romans 8:26-27	Likewise, the Spirit also helpeth our infirmities: for we know not what we should pray for as we ought: but the Spirit itself maketh intercession for us with groanings which cannot be uttered. And he that searcheth the hearts knoweth what is the mind of the Spirit, because he maketh intercession for the saints according to the will of God.

For the Closet: The Holy Spirit helps us in our inabilities to pray to God as we should and translates our inarticulate groans into a language understood by our Father. He knows our hearts' desires. The purpose of God's prayers is designed for a particular moment in His time. Hence, we must be willing to allow the Holy Spirit to connect us to God's sovereignty, leading us in prayer, orchestrated by God's will.

Week	Scripture	Text
4	Psalm 100:4	Enter into his gates with thanksgiving, and into His courts with praise: be thankful unto Him, and bless His name.

For the Closet: Where would we be if we did not abide in His dwelling place? It is a privilege to have a secret place to bless the name of the Lord. We should enter the prayer closet thanking Him for the dwelling place, and praise our Maker for the blessed splendor of His presence.

NOTES

_____

_____

_____

_____

_____

_____

_____

_____

_____

_____

_____

_____

_____

_____

_____

_____

_____

_____

_____

New Beginnings: Our Beginnings in Him (Jesus Christ)

Do you remember the first time you surrendered your life to Jesus and how good you felt when you were freed from the bondage of sin that held you captive? Do you remember how the sky seemed bluer, birds sang louder, and everything around you seemed bigger and better? Yes, you were just glad to be alive and for the first time, you really knew what true love meant…Jesus and the Father! God's desire is for us to return to humble beginnings, praying for fresh new encounters with Him daily.

Week	Scripture	Text
1	1 Chronicles 17:9	Also I will ordain a place for My people Israel, and will plant them, and they shall dwell in their place, and shall be moved no more; neither shall the children of wickedness waste them any more, as at the beginning.

For the Closet: God has had our back since the beginning, long before we knew Him. Let's humble ourselves and seek His presence in a place of His choosing. Thus, we can forgive and move above and beyond things said or done in the past, that once offended us.

Week	Scripture	Text
2	Lamentations 3:21-23	This I recall to my mind, therefore have I hope. It is of the LORD's mercies that we are not consumed, because His compassions fail not. They are new every morning: great is Thy faithfulness.

For the Closet: Even if we have invoked unfortunate consequences through ungodly actions, we must remember our Father who got us out of the mess the first time, and exercise humility, pray, and seek His presence. Then we experience God's tender mercies, fresh and anew as in the beginning.

Week	Scripture	Text
3	John1:1,2, 14	In the beginning was the Word, and the Word was with God, and the Word was God. The same was in the beginning with God. And the Word was made flesh, and dwelt among us (and we beheld his glory, the glory as of the only begotten of the Father) full of grace and truth.

For the Closet: God clothed himself in humanity and became subject to sufferings and mortality through His son Jesus Christ, with the divine purpose to forgive our sins and save mankind. Because of His unmerited favor, we know of a truth. God answers prayers for those who believe in Jesus (God's Word). NOW we understand the significance of praying in the name of Jesus.

Week	Scripture	Text
4	Revelations 1:8	I am Alpha and Omega, the beginning and the ending, saith the Lord, which is, and which was, and which is to come, the Almighty.

For the Closet: The book of revelations provides insight on how our story ends, while simultaneously unveiling our true beginnings. Jesus reveals He is truly the spoken and active Word of God, and in Him all things were made, are made, and still more to come. We must ask God to reveal the totality of His presence in the knowledge of the revelation of Jesus Christ.

NOTES

_____

_____

_____

_____

_____

_____

_____

_____

_____

_____

_____

_____

_____

_____

_____

_____

_____

_____

MONTH 4

Revelation of Christ: Wisdom, Understanding & Knowledge

God the Father drew us to Himself and revealed His loving salvation—Jesus Christ. It is Jesus that re-presents us to the Father. The Holy Spirit choreographs our relationship to God through the Son, constantly updating us with fresh knowledge, hidden wisdom, and refreshing our understanding, by sharpening our supernatural connections. However, we must allow the Holy Spirit to take the lead in our spiritual dance, by preparing ourselves in the prayer closet. Hence, we'll never miss a step and are always guaranteed to dance, in the joy of both the Father and the Son.

Week	Scripture	Text
1	Matthew 16:16–17	And Simon Peter answered and said, Thou art the Christ, the Son of the living God. And Jesus answered and said unto him, Blessed art thou, Simon Barjona: for flesh and blood hath not revealed it unto thee, but my Father which is in heaven.

For the Closet: It is our Father who initially reveals His son, Jesus the anointed one, to us. From this revelation, we discover that ALL of God's secret things are known to us, but we must stay connected to Him, by praying in the name of the only son He freely gave for us.

Week	Scripture	Text
2	Ephesians 1:17–18	That the God of our Lord Jesus Christ, the Father of glory, may give unto you the spirit of wisdom and revelation in the knowledge of Him: The eyes of your understanding being enlightened; that ye may know what is the hope of His calling, and what the riches of the glory of His inheritance in the saints.

For the Closet: Pray that God gives us the breath of wisdom, relative to His goodness, and unveil the divine knowledge of Christ in our lives. Through spiritual eyes, we see God's desired expectation of His call on our lives, and our inherited riches illuminated through the Son in Him.

Week	Scripture	Text
3	1 Corinthians 2:16	For who hath known the mind of the Lord, that he may instruct him? But we have the mind of Christ.

For the Closet: It is the Holy Ghost that teaches us the things that exist in the mind of Christ. During prayer, allow Him to reveal the things of God by emptying ourselves of *natural* thoughts, and let God fill us to the brim with *supernatural* thoughts of Christ.

Week	Scripture	Text
4	Hebrews 13:8	Jesus Christ the same yesterday, and today, and forever.

For the Closet: Jesus is the anointed Son of God; a manifested expression of God's living Word, which has never changed and remains fixed throughout eternity. If we build our prayers upon this eternal foundation, we will forever remain in the presence of God.

NOTES

_____

_____

_____

_____

_____

_____

_____

_____

_____

_____

_____

_____

_____

_____

_____

_____

_____

_____

_____

_____

_____

_____

MONTH 5

Passion of Christ: God's Will in Action

Jesus is God's Word manifested in the flesh, which is God's will in action. Therefore, in order for us to activate the manifestation of God's will, we must follow Jesus as he followed God, which is to passionately do, say, and pray the things of God. God's passion was to give "His only begotten son," Jesus' passion was to do the will of the Father, and our passion is to do God's will revealed through active prayer in the name of Jesus.

Week	Scripture	Text
1	Luke 4:18-19	The Spirit of the Lord is upon me, because he hath anointed me to preach the gospel to the poor; he hath sent me to heal the brokenhearted, to preach deliverance to the captives, and recovering of sight to the blind, to set at liberty them that are bruised, to preach the acceptable year of the Lord.

Dr. Shelia R. Lewis

For the Closet: In the prayer closet we are given the anointing of the Holy Spirit, to passionately do the things Jesus did, which draws people and ourselves, close to God.

Week	Scripture	Text
2	Luke 22:42 & 44	Saying, Father, if thou be willing, remove this cup from me: nevertheless not my will, but thine, be done…And being in an agony he prayed more earnestly: and his sweat was as it were great drops of blood falling down to the ground.

For the Closet: Sometimes circumstances in life cause us to want God to remove its nuances and can even affect our prayer lives. However, we must surrender our will to God and purpose to pray the faithful Word of God, even in the midst of our circumstances.

Week	Scripture	Text
3	Acts 1:3	To whom also he showed himself alive after his passion by many infallible proofs, being seen of them forty days, and speaking of the things pertaining to the kingdom of God.

For the Closet: After the crucifixion of Jesus, He reappeared to the Apostles to spend time with them, revealing more about the Kingdom of God. Open the door of your closet when Jesus knocks and ask Him to reveal the things of God's kingdom, which enables you to partake in the advancement of God's will on earth as it is in Heaven.

Week	Scripture	Text
4	Romans 10:9-10	That if thou shalt confess with thy mouth the Lord Jesus, and shalt believe in thine heart that God hath raised him from the dead, thou shalt be saved. For with the heart man believeth unto righteousness; and with the mouth confession is made unto salvation.

For the Closet: God delivers, saves, and preserves us if we simply confess that Jesus is our Lord and Savior, and have unyielding confidence that God made us righteous through His son. Pray for God to resound within our souls that the righteousness we became was bought and paid for through Jesus; we did not save ourselves. Then with humbled souls, we can boldly and passionately declare JESUS CHRIST IS LORD!!!

Dr. Shelia R. Lewis

NOTES

_____

_____

_____

_____

_____

_____

_____

_____

_____

_____

_____

_____

_____

_____

_____

_____

_____

_____

MONTH 6

Healing & Wholeness: Faith in God is Wholeness for God's People

Believing that God keeps His Word is profound when we pray in the name of Jesus. Consider that Jesus is God's Word and "in His name" is more than a closing phrase to end our prayer sessions. Once we truly experience His power and authority, we align our spirit to God's Spirit, and our soul and body follow. In other words, we are made whole, sanctified, and blameless simply because we believe it was through this Lamb that we have access to the Holy Kingdom.

Week	Scripture	Text
1	Isaiah 53:5	Surely he hath borne our griefs, and carried our sorrows: yet we did esteem him stricken, smitten of God, and afflicted. But He was wounded for our transgressions, He was bruised for our iniquities: the chastisement of our peace was upon Him; and with His stripes we are healed.

Dr. Shelia R. Lewis

For the Closet: Jesus took the beating for the crooked, sinful paths we take in life...from Adam-to-us-to-future generations. No matter how broken society appears, we can pray for wholeness in the knowledge that we are healed because of the beating Jesus took for each of us.

Week	Scripture	Text
2	James 5:14–16	Is any sick among you? Let him call for the elders of the church; and let them pray over him, anointing him with oil in the name of the Lord: And the prayer of faith shall save the sick, and the Lord shall raise him up; and if he have committed sins, they shall be forgiven him.

For the Closet: We are called by God to pray for the healing of bodies and souls of those who can't pray for themselves. Therefore, it is imperative that we pray for the Holy Spirit to keep us in God's will, because a sick world depends on our healthy relationship with God.

Week	Scripture	Text
3	Matthew 14:35–36	And when the men of that place had knowledge of him, they sent out into all that country round about, and brought unto him all that were diseased; And besought him that they might only touch the hem of his garment: and as many as touched were made perfectly whole.

> **For the Closet**: The knowledge of Jesus will lead men to bring their diseased state to His footstool. We must pray that God opens the eyes of men to understand that just a touch from Jesus is enough to heal every unhealthy thing in their lives.

Week	Scripture	Text
4	1 Thessalonians 5:23-25	And the very God of peace sanctify you wholly; and I pray God your whole spirit and soul and body be preserved blameless unto the coming of our Lord Jesus Christ. Faithful is he that calleth you, who also will do it. Brethren, pray for us.

> **For the Closet**: Our relationship with God requires total commitment to Him, i.e., spirit, soul, and body. Let us follow Paul's example and pray that God preserves us wholly as we anticipate the second coming of Jesus Christ our Lord and Savior.

NOTES

_____

_____

_____

_____

_____

_____

_____

_____

_____

_____

_____

_____

_____

_____

_____

_____

_____

_____

_____

_____

MONTH 7

Heaviness: Replaced With the Oil of Joy, Comforter & the Garment of Praise

Wouldn't it be marvelous if life was ALWAYS "peachy creamy" after we accepted Jesus Christ as our Lord and Savior? Unfortunately, for our earth-suited creature, yet fortunate for our spiritual being, we can praise God in the oil of the Holy Spirit and in anticipation of the better promise of eternal life in Jesus. Through consistent prayer, the heavenly mix (Oil of Joy, Comforter and Garment of Praise) freely given overcomes heaviness in our earth suit. Sons and daughters of God, pray for the saints that they also pray and overcome heaviness and magnify God's praise and glory.

Week	Scripture	Text
1	Psalm 119:28	My soul melteth for heaviness: strengthen thou me according unto thy word
For the Closet: In several places in the Old Testament, God is often called a Rock and Strength. When our souls begin to stoop from the weight of the world, pray the promised words of God, overflowing within the Holy Scriptures, and lift up your inner man and become strong.		

Dr. Shelia R. Lewis

Week	Scripture	Text
2	Isaiah 61:3	To appoint unto them that mourn in Zion, to give unto them beauty for ashes, the oil of joy for mourning, the garment of praise for the spirit of heaviness; that they might be called trees of righteousness, the planting of the LORD, that he might be glorified.

For the Closet: Jesus cited Isaiah 61:1-2 in the synagogue in Luke 4:18 concerning the anointing of the Lord upon himself. Isaiah 61:3 further describes how the anointing produces joy, is cloaked with praise, and plants God's people as immovable trees for His glory. Let us pray to forever remain in the beauty of His holiness.

Week	Scripture	Text
3	John 14:15-18	If ye love me, keep my commandments. And I will pray the Father, and he shall give you another Comforter, that he may abide with you for ever; Even the Spirit of truth; whom the world cannot receive, because it seeth him not, neither knoweth him: but ye know him; for he dwelleth with you, and shall be in you. I will not leave you comfortless: I will come to you.

For the Closet: Jesus prayed to the Father for the Holy Spirit to help us until Jesus' second coming. Because we demonstrate obedience through our love for Him: He has not orphaned us. Our spirit welcomes the warm encounter of God's presence in our daily communion (prayer) with Him.

Week	Scripture	Text
4	1 Peter 1:5-7	Who are kept by the power of God through faith unto salvation ready to be revealed in the last time. Wherein ye greatly rejoice, though now for a season, if need be, ye are in heaviness through manifold temptations: That the trial of your faith, being much more precious than of gold that perisheth, though it be tried with fire, might be found unto praise and honour and glory at the appearing of Jesus Christ

For the Closet: Prayer is vital in our faith walk with God. Through our prayerful relationship with God, we rejoice in all life's circumstances because we know our Lord and Savior Jesus Christ commends the testing of our faith, when we endure in His name.

NOTES

_____

_____

_____

_____

_____

_____

_____

_____

_____

_____

_____

_____

_____

_____

_____

_____

_____

_____

MONTH 8

Unnecessary Weight: Exercising Spiritual Liberty

When we follow Jesus, our eyes are fixed on Him from the starting gate to the finish line. Although the world is full of many falsehoods, exercised through the mouths of the enemy's imps, we know that the ultimate Overcomer (Jesus) dwells on the inside of us. Hence, to effectively run the race, we shed ALL unnecessary weight before we begin. In doing so, we invoke the Father's presence who sees us through the race, yet waits at the finish line to reward us with the spiritual gift of freedom from ALL bondages of the world.

Week	Scripture	Text
1	Hebrews 12:1(b)	...Let us lay aside every weight, and the sin which doth so easily beset us, and let us run with patience the race that is set before us
For the Closet: Holding on to past sins adds extra weight and slow us down in our Christian race. We must endure the race in the revelation knowledge that all we do is orchestrated from start to finish in Jesus Christ.		

Dr. Shelia R. Lewis

Week	Scripture	Text
2	Galatians 2:4	And that because of false brethren unawares brought in, who came in privily to spy out our liberty which we have in Christ Jesus, that they might bring us into bondage

For the Closet: Pray that we not only humble our souls unto the Lord, but that He provides us the discernment to recognize and avoid doctrines other than the foundational doctrine of Jesus Christ. For He (Christ) alone is the Chief Corner Stone fitly placed by God Himself.

Week	Scripture	Text
3	Hebrews 2:14(b)-15	…that through death he might destroy him that had the power of death, that is, the devil; And deliver them who through fear of death were all their lifetime subject to bondage

For the Closet: Jesus has destroyed the one who had the power of death, so now we are free to walk in the liberty of life everlasting. Bind the devil's suggestive notions of death that once caused fear, and loose the resurrecting power in every aspect of your life in the name of Jesus.

Week	Scripture	Text
4	1 John 4:4	Ye are of God, little children, and have overcome them: because greater is he that is in you, than he that is in the world.

For the Closet: We overcome the weight of the world by the weight of God's glory through His Son. Continue to pray that God illuminates the power of Christ from within, for us and for our brethren.

NOTES

MONTH 9

Overcoming Idleness: Praying for a Fervent Spirit

God promised us that He would hear from heaven and heal our land if we meet some pre-existing conditions, one of which is to seek His face (presence). Jesus passionately gave His life for us to have a relationship with God. Our prayer life is imminent in the process of seeking the presence of God, so never quit and God will ensure the rivers in your belly continuously flow for Him.

Week	Scripture	Text
1	Isaiah 60:1	Arise, shine; for thy light is come, and the glory of the LORD is risen upon thee.
For the Closet: God will manifest all good things for us, but we must be active in acquiring these things. The first step is to arise, "Get up," pray and ask God to lead us in the activity required to come into whatsoever He has for us.		

Week	Scripture	Text
2	Acts 18:25	This man *(Apollos)* was instructed in the way of the Lord; and being fervent in the spirit, he spake and taught diligently the things of the Lord, knowing only the baptism of John.

For the Closet: Even though Apollos preached God the Father in the baptism of John, he was on fire to share what he knew. This prompted Aquila and Priscilla to expound unto him the way of God more perfectly, i.e., the gospel of Jesus Christ. As a result, Apollos publicly convinced Jews that Jesus was Christ. Let us pray that God increases our demonstration of spiritual passion to others, bringing them to Him through Christ.

Week	Scripture	Text
3	Romans 12:11-12	Not slothful in business; fervent in spirit; serving the Lord; Rejoicing in hope; patient in tribulation; continuing instant in prayer

For the Closet: Because of time spent in prayer, we enter the world daily with a passion to share God's Word. It is the illumination of joy others see, regardless of life circumstances, that makes them desire this unquenchable fire.

Week	Scripture	Text
4	Hebrews 6:12	That ye be not slothful, but followers of them who through faith and patience inherit the promises.
For the Closet: Jesus Christ is the same yesterday, today, and forever. Let us fervently reinforce our faith and patience through a constant action that has stood the test of time—PRAYER.		

NOTES

_____

_____

_____

_____

_____

_____

_____

_____

_____

_____

_____

_____

_____

_____

_____

_____

_____

_____

_____

_____

Humility: Praying With an Humble Spirit

Total submission to God is humility and it requires us to leave all our cares with Him. Therefore, enter the prayer closet as a child willing to tell the Father all about your experiences since the last time you were with Him. Although He already knows our seats of passion, our caring Father wants us to know that He desires to HEAR our openly shared confessions. This is how He knows we trust Him in all our ways.

Week	Scripture	Text
1	2 Chronicles 7:14	If my people, which are called by my name, shall humble themselves, and pray, and seek my face, and turn from their wicked ways; then will I hear from heaven, and will forgive their sin, and will heal their land.

For the Closet: God knows we sometimes miss the mark. However, He is eager to hear, forgive, and even heal us when we seek Him in true humility. Turn from things unlike Him, and turn TO Him.

Dr. Shelia R. Lewis

Week	Scripture	Text
2	Isaiah 57:15	For thus saith the high and lofty One that inhabiteth eternity, whose name is Holy; I dwell in the high and holy place, with him also that is of a contrite and humble spirit, to revive the spirit of the humble, and to revive the heart of the contrite ones.

For the Closet: It is when our will is truly broken and a penitent heart, that God can mold us according to His will. Humble yourself when you pray, and allow God to shape you according to His Divine nature.

Week	Scripture	Text
3	Matthew 18:4	Whosoever therefore shall humble himself as this little child, the same is greatest in the kingdom of heaven

For the Closet: Let us remember the days of our childhood, care free and depending on a loved one to provide for us. As born again Christians, let's humble ourselves as spiritual children trusting in the Father to provide what's best for us according to His will.

Week	Scripture	Text
4	1 Peter 5:6-7	Humble yourselves therefore under the mighty hand of God, that he may exalt you in due time: Casting all your care upon him; for he careth for you.

For the Closet: Pray that God teaches us the spirit of humility by which we cast life cares upon Him. Then God will give us a prayer life that incites His powerful Spirit to do all that we can ever ask or think.

NOTES

_____

_____

_____

_____

_____

_____

_____

_____

_____

_____

_____

_____

_____

_____

_____

_____

_____

MONTH 11

Leadership: Ensamples to the Flock

The scriptures are filled with examples, both good and evil, that teach us what to do and what not to do. An ensample is also an example, but is more of an outward manifestation of something inward, shaped (emblem) of what is higher. Hence, we are types of Christ (Christians) and representatives of Him. Our conversation, behavior, and character should mirror Him when we willingly provide oversight and tenderly care for those God has placed in our midst.

Week	Scripture	Text
1	Joshua 5:13b–14	…and Joshua went unto him, and said unto him, Art thou for us, or for our adversaries? And he said, Nay; but as captain of the host of the LORD am I now come. And Joshua fell on his face to the earth, and did worship, and said unto him, What saith my Lord unto his servant?

For the Closet: Joshua was prepared to go to battle when the Lord himself showed up to *take charge*. This should be our intent when we enter into prayer with the Lord. That is, we need to allow Him to take over and provide guidance and direction according to His Divine will.

Week	Scripture	Text
2	Matthew 15:14	Let them alone: they be blind leaders of the blind. And if the blind lead the blind, both shall fall into the ditch.

For the Closet: Jesus warns his disciples to stay away from leaders that follow the traditions of man and stray from the oracles of God. Likewise, we must pray for God to provide us with humility to do and teach His commandments.

Week	Scripture	Text
3	Hebrews 13:7-8	Remember them which have the rule over you, who have spoken unto you the word of God: whose faith follow, considering the end of their conversation. Jesus Christ the same yesterday, and to day, and for ever.

For the Closet: If we stay focused on Jesus we will not become blind nor follow blind leaders. Our conduct and conversation will illuminate Jesus the chief Shepard that will ALWAYS lead us, and lead others to our Heavenly Father. Thank God for a never changing Jesus!

Week	Scripture	Text
4	1 Peter 5:2–3	Feed the flock of God which is among you, taking the oversight thereof, not by constraint, but willingly; not for filthy lucre, but of a ready mind; Neither as being lords over God's heritage, but being ensamples to the flock.

For the Closet: As leaders of God's flock we are charged as overseers to provide spiritual food to nourish their souls. Hence, we must allow God to fashion us after our chief cornerstone, Jesus Christ. A continual prayer life ensures that we tenderly nourish the flock according to the heavenly pattern revealed to us in the prayer closet.

NOTES

_____

_____

_____

_____

_____

_____

_____

_____

_____

_____

_____

_____

_____

_____

_____

_____

_____

MONTH 12

Blessings for the Children

A healthy prayer life blesses our children (both natural and spiritual) based on the promises of God mentioned throughout the scriptures. Never forget that we also are products of prayer, by those who went before us. Although we are sons and daughters of God, we must also remember that it is with a child's heart and total submission to God, which allows us to enter the kingdom and receive what God has for us according to His good will and purpose.

Week	Scripture	Text
1	Genesis 22:17-18	That in blessing I will bless thee (*Abraham*), and in multiplying I will multiply thy seed as the stars of the heaven, and as the sand which is upon the sea shore; and thy seed shall possess the gate of his enemies; And in thy seed shall all the nations of the earth be blessed; because thou hast obeyed my voice.

Dr. Shelia R. Lewis

For the Closet: We too are entitled to the blessings of Abraham, whereby our offspring are blessed because of our obedience to the voice of God. The more time we spend with God in our prayer closets, the more familiar we are with His voice. Get to know Him more and bless our children.

Week	Scripture	Text
2	Proverbs 20:7	The just man walketh in his integrity: his children are blessed after him.

For the Closet: Pray that we walk in the innocence and fullness of God in our body, soul, and spirit. In doing so, we bless the children of our present day and those in the future.

Week	Scripture	Text
3	Acts 3:25	Ye are the children of the prophets, and of the covenant which God made with our fathers, saying unto Abraham, And in thy seed shall all the kindreds of the earth be blessed.

For the Closet: We are the children of the covenant between God and Abraham, and first in line after the Son of God—Jesus Christ. Let us pray for God to reveal Himself to us as *our* loving, caring, and sharing Heavenly Father, in whom we confidently place our trust.

Week	Scripture	Text
4	Mark 10:14b-16	Suffer the little children to come unto me, and forbid them not: for of such is the kingdom of God. Verily I say unto you, Whosoever shall not receive the kingdom of God as a little child, he shall not enter therein. And he took them up in his arms, put his hands upon them, and blessed them.

For the Closet: Enter into the prayer closet as a child expecting Jesus to embrace and bless you. Through complete child-like submission, He will place His hands upon you and present you to our Father.

Dr. Shelia R. Lewis

NOTES

_____

_____

_____

_____

_____

_____

_____

_____

_____

_____

_____

_____

_____

_____

_____

_____

_____

_____

_____

_____

_____